FROM SURVIVAL TO REVIVAL

By Joseph Pero

ISBN-13: 978-0692333709
Library of Congress Control Number: 2014956806

Published in the United States by:
King and Queen Publishing, LLC
www.kingandqueenpublishingllc.com
services@kingandqueenpublishingllc.com
Hon. Lyfe Prince blackking@kingandqueenpublishingllc.com
Tiffany L. Prince blackqueen@kingandqueenpublishingllc.com

Printed in the United States

King and Queen Publishing

I dedicate this book to my maternal grandmother, Ernetta Myers, who was a devout Christian who prayed for me to become a disciple of Christ. Your prayers have been answered, Grandma (although a little late!). I know she is smiling in Heaven!

Acknowledgments

I would like to thank my friend, Bruce Edwards, for his valuable input. He was one of the first people to read the manuscript, and he made valuable contributions as to its content. I would also like to thank my friend, Todd Abbey, who encouraged me to write the book. Finally, I would like to thank Tiffany Rucker of King and Queen Publishing, LLC for believing in the material and having faith in me as a writer. Thank you, Tiffany!

Foreword

Many people seek to find a way to deal with the struggles in their lives. In order to remain alive through life's obstacles you have to understand and be wise to your options in order to overcome. When I met Joseph within the organization that he and I both are affiliated with I had no idea that he had written such an impeccable piece of work.

Joseph presented his book to me as a review. He was very aware of the work he held in his hand, however he had no clue the impact his work could possibly have on someone's life and neither did I. The title itself is thought provoking.

At first glance you will see this book as being just another self-help book, I know I did. What you hold in your hand now, is a collection of clear, concise, thought provoking principles.

After I performed my first review of part one I was instantly anticipating part two and what it entailed. This book is broken down into two parts and each part is broken down into principles, which allows you to break each principle down to a clearer relatable understanding. Joseph shares his experience as a non-believer, his journey to becoming a believer and then his new experience as a believer. He correlates the non-believer as being in Survival Mode and the believer as being in Revival Mode. His presentation is candid and intriguing.

You will learn some things about yourself. You will also want to change some things about yourself. You will enjoy every page, every principle and the journey in itself. The end result is that you will find exactly what you are looking for if you follow the blueprint of principles and take each step as they are presented.

Honorable Tiffany L. Rucker
King and Queen Publishing, LLC

" ... This book gives the reader a practical comparison between worldly living, and living with a greater purpose in mind. The author's personal approach is genuine and dares to ask each of us to draw our own conclusion. You will find the book challenging, convicting and pointing us away from the "wing it" lifestyle that so plagues American culture today."

Rev. Bob Chaffee, Men's Pastor, Grace Church, Middleburg Heights, OH

" ... The Christian struggling to live for Christ should read From Survival to Revival. It is unlike any other Christian help book, because it has practical and simple truths, written to be easily understood. The methods can be applied to the Christian's personal life and their experiences, without a dictionary or interpretation. After 40 years, I've finally found a book that I can recommend to any Christian including the well trained."

Bruce Edwards

PART ONE: SURVIVAL MODE

Did you ever get asked the question, "How are you?" or "How's it going?" The traditional answer is usually "fine" or "good". Growing up, I always had to be a little different. Never satisfied with the pat answer, and also realizing that people really do not want to hear the truth, I came up with the coy remark, "I'm Surviving!", which naturally leads to the remark, "It's better than the alternative." Upon reflection of my life, I now realize that all I have been doing is just surviving. I have barely been living. While I have a good job, live in a nice home, and drive a nice car, I have just been getting by with the bare essentials. I don't have a family to share things with, and I don't really feel that I am living to my fullest potential as a human being. I live a solitary life for the most part. I have friends, but most of them are married or have children, which constitutes a major portion of their lives. I have my pets, but they don't talk to me, unless it's feeding time, and then I'll get an earful. I just do my work, come home, play with my pets, and then veg out in front of my television, where I find myself living vicariously through the characters that I watch on my TV. In fact, my dream life is far more exciting than my real life, making it sometimes difficult to wake up in the morning. In fact, there are days that I just want to roll over and continue dreaming. However, my pets are always around to remind me that I have responsibilities to meet, so I grudgingly get up to start my day. Only recently I have come to the realization that I have been in Survival Mode for all these many years.

I have come to believe that I am not alone in this. A majority of Americans are living "lives of quiet desperation", as the old Pink Floyd song went. Many of us are living in Survival Mode, as evident by the rise of bankruptcies, foreclosures, and job losses to overseas operations or stiff competition in many industries. We are barely able to make ends meet, and we find ourselves sliding further and further into debt. Compound this with worldwide terrorist attacks and natural disasters, it is easy to see how people can become discouraged, depressed, and angry by life's twists and turns. Growing up, we all had dreams and aspirations of what we wanted to do with our lives. However, as time marched on, and the world changed along with it, those dreams evaporated, and the hopes of childhood became lost to the realities of life. To many of us, just surviving seemed like a good thing. I no longer share this view.

I want everyone to know that I refuse to continue to "live like a refugee" (as that Tom Petty song went), and accept the meager existence that had kept me held down and trapped by these circumstances that fill up the hours of the day. I no longer want to be a Survivor. Instead, I want to live life to its fullest potential, just as God created me to live. I want to utilize my talents and skills to their fullest abilities, just as God intended me to use them. I want to create a new life for myself and make a difference in people's life, just as Jesus has done for me. I want to play a major role in God's kingdom, and I want to help those also stuck in Survivor Mode to get unstuck.

This book, **From Survival to Revival**, is designed to help the reader to understand these two very different modes of living, and how someone can simply flip a switch and change the circumstances surrounding them just by making the right choices in life. To be honest with you, I chose to live the life of a Survivor, not because I was a glutton for punishment, but I became comfortable with my life. Often times, we find ourselves living in a comfortable rut, in a nice little safety zone. Sometimes, we do not realize that just by making a few slight detours along the way of life, we could be setting ourselves up to fail and not receive the glory. Well, I am here to testify that this does not have to be a permanent situation, and that God will be there to accept you into his kingdom once you make the choice to receive his grace. Once you do make the choice, then you are ready to move into the Revival Zone. My brother is a paramedic, and when they revive someone, especially after a cardiac arrest, that person becomes alive again. In a spiritual sense, when you accept Jesus Christ as your savior, you are born again as a new person in the eyes of God. Once you move into the Revival Zone, your life will take on a whole new meaning. Is it easy? Not quite. You will have to give up (or surrender) your old ways, and learn a whole new way of thinking and handling situations. You will have to give up your comfort zone, and prepare for challenges you did not know you would face. Is it worth it? Why, of course it is!. It's far better than living day to day, paycheck to paycheck, hand to mouth. You will be glad that you did!

Now, this book is broken down into two sections. The first section is what the Survival Mode looks like. The second part is how to switch to Revival Mode, once you accept that you are a Survivor just like I was. As you read the first section, I want to let you know that you will find yourself experiencing three different responses that I call AAA. The first response will be **Awareness**, which takes place almost immediately upon reading the descriptions of what a Survivor is. The next response is **Acknowledgment**, which helps you to digest the information you are being given. The third, and last response, will be **Acceptance**. Only when you can fully accept what you have read as truth, then you are able to move onto the next section, involving the Revival Mode. If you cannot accept the notion of where you are as a Survivor, then the next section will not be worth reading. If you are too stubborn to accept these simple truths, then how will you be able to accept the divine truths laid out in the next section? I tell you this now because I do not believe in pulling punches. I am going to be as direct, as honest, and as in-your-face as I like to be treated. If you cannot accept such blunt honesty, then there are whole sections of self-help books that you can read at your public library or a bookstore. These books may purport to help you, but once you get past the flowery jargon and subtle tones, you might find yourself as frustrated as I was, making small but minor changes that lack the substantial gain you expected to make in the first place. However, if you are willing to work with me, you will find that the information that you will be reading will open your eyes like mine were. You will then be ready to move your life to the next level, beyond your comfort zone and into a new way of living. Trust me, you will not be sorry!

What I have done is broken down the word SURVIVAL into 8 different categories. You may be familiar with some, but very antagonistic toward others. Again, it is important to accept ALL of these categories before moving forward. You may not like it, but who said you had to. Remember, your ability to accept the following notions are directly proportionate to your ability to accept Christ into your life. The more stubborn you are, the less able God will be to work in your life. Keep that in mind as you go through these categories, because some will be harder to accept than others.

SELF-CENTEREDNESS

Let's face facts...we are selfish creatures at heart. Now, some of us don't want to be, but when push comes to shove, it's every man for himself. We are born this way. When we were children, we only cared about our own needs. As teenagers, we were only concerned about being accepted by our friends and peers. As adults, we only care about the size of our paychecks and how many weeks of vacation time we will receive. We live for the weekends, and dread Monday mornings. Now, we do care about our children and our friends and our families, but when we talk about caring for others outside of our sphere of influence, we may donate some money and give lip service to a cause. We practice NIMBY politics (Not In My Back Yard) when it comes to new developments that may help the community as a whole. We are more concerned about the property value to our home instead of the value of life of the community as a whole. Of all the categories, this is the hardest for most people to accept. I was the same way myself. I cared about people, and I wanted to do good things for others, but my actions did not follow my good intentions. I had to take a hard look at myself to finally accept that I was behaving in selfish ways most of the time. Even today, I find myself falling back into these bad habits. However, once you are aware and acknowledge these habits, you are more likely to strike them down when they rear their ugly heads.

Self-centeredness has been enculturated into us since birth. We are a competitive society, where only the strong survive, and it's every man for himself. To be a winner in the game of life, someone else has to lose. "To the Victor comes the Spoils" is the mantra of business today. Even our myths and legends are full of stories of fighting and winning against all odds. For many of us, Surrender is for the weak. Now contrast this sentiment to Christianity, which teaches us that we are to surrender to God's will, and that the meek shall inherit the earth. The two viewpoints are almost polar opposites to one another. Although we say we are a Christian society, we definitely do not practice what we preach! So please do not take offense to the notion that Survivors are selfish, because that is what has been ingrained into us by society. There is nobody to blame, but that does not mean we should continue to act this way. We must acknowledge and accept our selfish ways before we can move forward in our lives.

NOTES

<u>NOTES</u>

NOTES

_____

_____

_____

_____

_____

_____

_____

_____

_____

_____

_____

_____

_____

_____

_____

NOTES

UNDISCIPLINED / UNFOCUSED

The second characteristic of a Survivor is that he or she is generally undisciplined or unfocused in their everyday life. I am a true testament to this fact, especially when it comes to financial matters. Over the years, I have accrued a great deal of debt, and my focus has been on eliminating my debt without having to undergo bankruptcy. However, I found myself growing impatient with the process, and I began looking for ways to create other revenue for myself. I discovered many opportunities and projects to work on, outside of my own business, and I kept telling myself if I complete this project, I would be able to pay off all my remaining debts. Unfortunately, I began to lose focus on my business, which suffered in the process, which inevitably led to more debts in the process. It has become a vicious cycle for me, and one that I am desperately trying to extricate myself from. No matter what the project was, or how hard I worked, it would backfire on me in one way or another. For example, I recently tried to help a friend with his project, a major real estate development project. I worked out a complete business plan for his group, and I set up a team of people to help me to implement the plan. I did not get paid for this work, as I would get paid once the project began. However, my friend never received the financing he needed for the project, so my work is gathering dust in someone's file cabinet. So after months of hard work and diligent research, I find myself in the same place I was at the beginning of this project. Actually, I find myself in a worst place, as my bills had accumulated, my own business suffered, and I can't ever get that time back again. Unfortunately, I can count one hand the number of similar projects that I have been involved with, getting the very same result. My mantra used to be, "If you throw enough mud against the wall, some of it is bound to stick!" In my case, the walls were caked in mud, but all I got was mud! None of my projects panned out for one reason or another, and this led me to be more frustrated. This also led me to get involved in projects that were highly speculative in nature.

The reason I am telling you this story is to show you how being unfocused and undisciplined can wreak havoc in your life if you are not careful. Even though I had debts, I should have focused my energies on my business, creating new revenue streams for that, instead of looking outside of it to accomplish my goals. Being undisciplined in my business caused it to suffer greatly. I also lacked focus on the part of getting involved in these projects. I would be involved in one project, and then I would be tempted to get involved into another project, which gave the illusion of getting bigger returns. It took me farther and farther away from my original intention of simply paying off my debts for good. As a Survivor, you find yourself being drawn into different things in the hopes of alleviating your situation, whatever that is. It is not uncommon for a Survivor to be drawn into "opportunities" that may or may not pan out. Sometimes Survivors are so desperate for some kind of relief, they will do almost anything if there is even a remote chance that the pain will go away. This is what I consider to be Unfocused. The bible talks about "A man cannot serve two Masters", and when you are unfocused, your energy is being scattered about like a shotgun blast. When you do not have the discipline to walk away from a project, no matter how tempting it may seem, you will see your effectiveness decrease accordingly. You become worthless in your pursuits, and risk becoming a burden to others. This is the problem behind being undisciplined or unfocused.

<u>NOTES</u>

_____

_____

_____

_____

_____

_____

_____

_____

_____

_____

_____

_____

_____

_____

_____

_____

_____

NOTES

NOTES

_____

_____

_____

_____

_____

_____

_____

_____

_____

_____

_____

_____

_____

_____

_____

_____

_____

<u>**NOTES**</u>

REACTIONARY

Did you ever go to the movies, and see a particularly disturbing scene, and everyone in the theater gasps or gags, whatever the case may be? What you are doing is reacting to your environment. Marketing people, movie producers, and other media manipulators try to gauge the customers' reactions, trying to create a 'buzz' for their products or services. From an early age, we are 'trained' to react to different stimuli and environmental conditions. By 'trained', I am talking about Conditional Responses. Like Pavlov's dogs, which salivated whenever they hear a bell, we are 'trained' to respond to stimuli in the same manner by our media. Whenever there is a sexy girl on the screen, you are going to get some type of reaction from the male gender. It may, at one time, been a natural response, but as we become more and more exposed to such scenarios, we become desensitized by what we are seeing. So the media creates a more tempting environment by which to cause a reaction, more sensational than before. A good example of this are video games. When I was growing up, we had Pac-man and Space Invaders, moving slowly on our screens, as we attempted to raise our score. Over time, we became bored by these types of games, leading video game designers to create more 'compelling" story lines for games, increasing the danger, the blood and gore, as well as the sexiness of the characters. Getting a high score was still the goal, but now it was more seductive for the game player not to lose interest in the game. The evening news is the same way. The TV station will give the viewer a teaser, designed to get you to watch the broadcast, usually showing the more sinister, darker side of our society. They report, almost with glee, the number of dead fighting men and women, trying to create the illusion that the battle is a lost cause. They try to entertain us with gossip and innuendo of our politicians and entertainers, exposing their problems to us. They do this just to create a reaction in us.

We live in a reactionary society, as plainly seen here. As Survivors, we learn to react in our environments. You go to the store, and the salesperson walks up to you and the first thing out of your mouth is "Just Looking". That is a reaction. There is nothing wrong with it, but you are reacting to the situation at hand. The same goes when you go to work, go to the doctor, or go to the zoo. Marketing research people have mounds and mounds of data to show how people react in different environments and different situations. You may think you are acting independently of others, but you are acting within the norm of accepted social behavior. In some ways, we are like the rat in a maze, trying to find his way to the cheese. You may not like this kind of analogy, but take a look at how people react to things on a daily basis. Go to the mall and sit on a bench, and over the course of a day, you will see behavior taking place that is both predictable and acceptable. I find it fascinating to watch people in an environment like this, because I can tell what people will do even before they do it. It may seem uncanny, but when it comes down to it, human behavior, for the most part, is not really that unpredictable.

Now, you are probably asking yourself, "How is this a Survivor trait?" It is really simple. It takes energy to think and respond to situations, and most people, especially Survivors, are too lazy to do this. Instead, it is easier to go with the flow and react to a situation. It requires little thinking and little energy, and then we can move on to the next thing we are doing. In a way, I think of it as a 'mental hiccup', as people don't think about getting hiccups, but when they do, they just try to live with it until it gets too disruptive to them. Until something becomes too uncomfortable for us, such as rising gasoline prices, we continue to act accordingly. When it does require action on our parts, we will wait to see how others respond first. That's why there are leaders and there are followers in life. The followers wait to see how the leaders respond, then act accordingly. However, if we ever want to get ourselves out of the Survivor

Zone, then we have to learn to become our own leaders, and respond, not react, to given situations that we may find ourselves in.

__NOTES__

NOTES

_____

_____

_____

_____

_____

_____

_____

_____

_____

_____

_____

_____

_____

_____

_____

_____

NOTES

NOTES

VICTIMIZATION

Survivors are victims of their own circumstances. They love being the victim, as they want to blame others for what happened to them. By blaming others, they refuse to accept responsibilities for their own actions (or inactions, as the case may be.) As a society, we like to coddle our victims, show them our compassion and support, especially in times of crisis. However, survivors are constantly in a state of crisis in their lives, and they look outside themselves to blame for their circumstances. Just take a look at our legal system, for example. We are a litigious society, constantly suing anyone or any institution for some form of restitution. We try to blame others for our misfortune, and we use the legal system to try to gain some kind of recognition for our blamelessness. A number of years ago, I remember McDonald's getting sued for millions of dollars when a lady spilled some hot coffee on herself while driving. It didn't matter that she shouldn't have been driving with hot coffee in her hand in the first place, but instead of taking responsibility for her own actions, she sought to shift the blame on the people who sold her the coffee in the first place. The ironic thing is that she won! I could not believe it. I am just waiting for the day a cellular phone company gets charged for vehicular homicide because someone crashed while talking to someone on a cell phone. Mark my word, it will happen.

It is my personal belief that people choose to be victims because it attracts attention to themselves. They want people to feel sorry for them, and they try to use the situation to their advantage. I find it morally repugnant to do this, and I'll tell you why. Let me use my own life as an example. I was stricken with Spinal Meningitis at the age of six weeks old. I survived the ordeal, as did the rest of my family. As a result of my illness, I became deaf in one ear. Over time, the hearing in my other ear began to deteriorate. My last checkup showed that I lost 80% of my hearing in my good ear, leaving me with very little hearing left. Now, I could feel sorry for myself, and look to government programs to support me, but I choose not to. In fact, very few people realize the extent of my hearing loss. I am not ashamed to tell people, if it comes out in casual conversation, but I am not going to wear it on my shirt, "Shout! I Can't Hear you!" In fact, I have prepared myself for the day when my hearing finally goes. I have learned to read lips, and I speak sign language. It may be a little rusty, as I don't use it much, but I still learned it. I also have the Close Captioning programmed on my television. With the advent of the Internet, I can send instant messages and emails to those around me. However, you would not be able to tell about my condition, because I refuse to draw attention to it. Someone with a Victim mindset would have used this situation for their own selfish means, and blamed others for the situation they are in. They would blame their parents, their environment, or even God for their problems. However, it is easier to accept what is and get on with your life than it is to constantly draw attention to your disability (at least for me, it was!) That way, I could focus my energies on the areas that I could control, instead of dwelling on what I couldn't. Now that doesn't mean I have never played the victim card, as there have been situations where I could use my hearing loss to my advantage. However, for the most part, I tried to keep my deafness to myself, refusing to draw attention to it.

NOTES

NOTES

_____

_____

_____

_____

_____

_____

_____

_____

_____

_____

_____

_____

_____

_____

_____

_____

_____

NOTES

NOTES

INSENSITIVITY

As Survivors, we are insensitive to the plights of others, especially those less fortunate than ourselves. Why? Because we are so wrapped up in our own problems and our own situations, we don't have the time, inclination, or capacity to truly feel for others. I know this is a strong statement, and it may even make you feel upset, but bear with me. First of all, I never said you were incapable of feeling compassion for others. However, it is not a priority in your life to feel that, at least while going through your own struggles. I have heard countless people say, in one form or another, that once he or she gets rich, or retires, or solves their own problems, then they will turn their attentions to others, donating whatever money, time, or material the other parties may need. Unfortunately, the Survivor never reaches this plateau of giving, as new situations and circumstances draw away their energy and attention from these matters. When it comes to this, I am as guilty as the next person. Even though my heart is in the right place, my actions do not follow accordingly. Let me give you an example. Recently, a friend of mine was mugged at work, and was very distraught about it. She called me late at night, waking me from a sound slumber. I recall being upset by the fact that I was woken up, but when she told me of the situation, I held my tongue. However, my voice and demeanor over the phone belied my displeasure. She sensed my impatience, and got very upset with me for not caring about what had happened. The truth was that I didn't, and that there was really nothing I can do anyway, the act was done. What she really needed, it would be later pointed out to me, was someone to listen to her and sympathize with her pain. Selfishly, all I could think about was getting back to sleep. I was terribly insensitive to her, and I later apologized to her, but the damage was already done.

I do not believe that this is an isolated case. All of us survivors tend to relate to things based on our worldly experience, and when something does not match our experience, we tend to come across as cold and unfeeling. It is very difficult for a Survivor to empathize with another's plight, especially when times are difficult for ourselves. This is not a condemnation, but an acknowledgment that we cannot be all things to all people, no matter how hard we try to act otherwise. It takes an exceptional person to behave in an empathetic and sensitive matter, and that is not what a Survivor is capable of.

NOTES

NOTES

_____

_____

_____

_____

_____

_____

_____

_____

_____

_____

_____

_____

_____

_____

_____

_____

_____

_____

<u>NOTES</u>

NOTES

<u>V</u>OLATILITY

On the flip side of the coin, Survivors are capable of volatile mood swings. At times, we can be angry and upset, while other times, we can be depressed and listless. We can be happy and excited one moment, then crying and complaining the next. For the Survivor, there really is not a happy medium. Mood swings are prevalent due to our reactive nature. As I stated early, we react to things. As such, the smallest infraction, no matter how insignificant, can trigger us off. I have always had a nasty temper, and the slightest discord could set me off royally. I am a terribly impatient person, so when something is not going as planned, I tend to get very upset and angry. As in the situation with my friend, I was angry because I was awaken in the middle of the night. Even though I did not vocalize my anger, she could sense my aggravation. It is a struggle for me to keep control of my anger, and I am trying to learn patience. Even though I can be patient dealing with equipment and computers and such, I can't say the same in regards to my dealings with people. Even though I like people (for the most part), I find it incredibly frustrating dealing with people who cannot keep up with me when I am working. In fact, I tell people I work in three modes:

SLOW ... FAST... or GET OUT OF MY WAY!

Of course, this does not bode well with people I am working with, and many of times I have been called derogatory names, some deservedly so. However, I tell you this not to gloat, but to demonstrate how volatile our emotions can be if we cannot learn to control them. This can destroy relationships, hurt feelings, and cause unnecessary pain to others if we are not careful. I have a friend who is going through some tough times right now, and when I talk with her, I never know what type of mood she'll be in. Sometimes, talking with her is like walking on eggshells. I love her, but sometimes being around her can be an exhausting experience. I never know if I will accidentally set her off, creating more problems. I continue to do so, as I want her to know that I support her unconditionally. Unfortunately, this is the norm for most Survivors, not the exception. These mood swings are caused by irritability, stress, frustration, and fear, with fear being the leading cause of mood swings. Which leads us to the next characteristic:

NOTES

NOTES

_____

_____

_____

_____

_____

_____

_____

_____

_____

_____

_____

_____

_____

_____

_____

_____

<u>NOTES</u>

<u>NOTES</u>

APPREHENSION

A big part of what drives a Survivor is FEAR. Fear is the lowest common denominator of all Survivors. It is this negative emotion that controls us more than any other characteristic listed above. In fact, you might say it is the causality of all the characteristics on this list. When we live in fear, we live with a stressful heart and a troubled soul. As survivors, we are constantly worrying about things around us. Our jobs, our homes, our livelihoods, our family and friends, and our environment can trigger off any kind of anxiety linked to fear.

There are several types of fear, and I will deal with the most common types associated with Survivors. They are as followed:

1. *Fear of Failure*
2. *Fear of Success*
3. *Fear of the Unknown*
4. *Fear of Looking Bad (Ridicule)*
5. *Fear of Loss*
6. *Fear of Death*

These are the most common of fears. There are others, but a Survivor faces these fears almost on a daily basis. These fears, these apprehensions, are what drains us of our energy, causes us to lose focus, and concentrate solely on ourselves. When we are in survival mode, we are literally gripped with fear. It is little wonder, then, that we are barely holding ourselves together. All of our energies are used to block and manage our fears, or at least avoid them. That is why Survivors live in a subsisting environment. How can we lead a life of potential if we are too busy dealing with our fears? For anyone trying to deal with fear, they know how exhausting and debilitating it can be.

Fear can even lead to illness and, worst yet, death. According to Dr. Don Colbert, author of the book **Deadly Emotions**, "Fear has been associated with a wide variety of diseases, including cardiovascular diseases and hypertension; digestive-tract diseases such as colitis, Crohn's disease, irritable bowel syndrome, and ulcers; headaches; and skin disorders such as psoriasis, eczema, and stress acne. Fear can cause a decreased immune response, which may lead to frequent infections or the development of deadly disease. Fear can precede a heart attack...or even death." Even though fears are psychological in nature, they can take a physiological form. If we are not able to get a better grip on our fears, then we could be signing our own death certificates!

As I stated earlier, over the past couple of years, I have amassed enormous debts. Because of this, I live with the fear of losing everything I own. Every morning, I half expect the mortgage company to foreclose on my house, or take away my car, or take all of my possessions. It is not a good place to be. All my energies center around how I can alleviate my debt load, thereby allowing me to concentrate on the things I want to work on. It is a major battle for me, and one that I hope to remedy one day soon. However, as long as I live in fear and apprehension, I may never get to see the light of day. As I struggle with these issues, I find myself unable to show compassion for others who are going through similar trials, even though I should. It also causes me to become angry with people, as I don't like being in the situation I find myself in. I also suffer from frequent headaches, which are very debilitating, to say the least. Yet, when someone asks how I'm doing, I tell them I am surviving, afraid to let them know how I am really doing. This is the life of a Survivor. If you are reading this book, this is your life as well.

<u>NOTES</u>

<u>NOTES</u>

NOTES

NOTES

LOW SELF ESTEEM

The last characteristic is self explanatory. When you are in Survival mode, it is hard to feel good about yourself. It's difficult to give
yourself pep talks, especially when your fears and apprehensions rear their
ugly heads. It's tough to feel as if nothing can stop you, when you know
there is a roadblock right around the corner to stop you in your tracks.
Your fear and anxiety are in the back of your mind, and the biggest fear
is looking like a failure in front of your family and friends. In my personal
case, I was laughed at as a child, due to my speech impediment. People
treated me like I was retarded, when I wasn't. In fact, I was smarter than
most of the people I grew up with. I was able to get rid of my speech
impediment, but I never got over being ridiculed by my peers. To this
day, I always wonder if people are laughing at me behind my back, or not
taking me seriously. I now know that this is an irrational fear, but it affects
my self-esteem regardless. Getting laughed at and ridiculed had been a
traumatic experience for me, and the scars have yet to truly heal. However, I am determined to overcome this fear and pain. Again, I do not
feel that I am alone in this. My friend, who I mentioned earlier, is a beautiful woman, yet when I tell her that, she becomes very defensive. She
doesn't believe she is beautiful, and that prevents her from accepting compliments from people, even people that love her. As Survivors, we will
readily accept criticisms from others, but we won't accept compliments
from them! One of life's little ironies...

As a Survivor, one of the most difficult things to do is express
yourself freely. The main reason why is that you are living in the shadow
of fear. You are afraid of being discovered, the truth about your situation
being exposed, and you are afraid of getting hurt once again. As such,
you walk around wearing a mask to hide your emotions, your fears, and
your struggles from outsiders. You may let close friends and family members peer behind the mask, but that is only for very personal reasons. To
express yourself freely is to expose yourself, and a Survivor knows that in

order to survive, one must keep things to themselves and hold tightly to what they fear most.

Now you are aware of the eight characteristics of a Survivor. They are as followed:

1. Self-centeredness
2. Undisciplined/Unfocused
3. Reactionary
4. Victimization
5. Insensitivity
6. Volatility
7. Apprehension
8. Low Self-esteem

Perhaps you recognize some of these qualities in yourself. Perhaps you are in a state of self-denial, like I was when I discovered these characteristics. However, as I said earlier, you need to accept these as truths if you are to proceed with the rest of the book. Without acceptance, you will deny yourself the full experience of being alive. Do not allow your fears and apprehensions keep you from living the life God intended for you to live. Don't allow your ego to get in the way of making a difference in your life and the lives of others. To truly be alive is the ultimate testimonial to God's grace. All it takes is to make a choice:

Do you want to stay in Survival Mode?
Or
Do you want to live in Revival Mode?

How you respond to the questions determine your ability to move in the right direction. Trust me when I say the answer you give will make all the difference in the world.

It's your choice...

<u>NOTES</u>

_____

_____

_____

_____

_____

_____

_____

_____

_____

_____

_____

_____

_____

_____

_____

_____

NOTES

<u>NOTES</u>

NOTES

Part Two: Revival Mode

Congratulations! You have made a wise and wonderful choice. By turning to this page, you have chose to create a new chapter in your life, one filled with hope, excitement, and potential! By reading this next section, you have decided that:

1. You have accepted that you are a Survivor, and that many, if not all, of the characteristics and attributes of a Survivor apply to you, in one degree or another, and...

2. You no longer wish to live the life of a Survivor, and you are willing to do whatever it takes to move on to the next level of living, and finally...

3. You want to live the life that God intended for you to live, and you desire to live to your fullest, best potential, whatever that may be!

(Editor's Note: We know from experience that some of you reading this may not have made any choice at all, but are curious to see what happens from here. If you haven't made this choice, please put this book down, and continue to live your life as you have done in the past. Don't worry...when you are truly ready, then you can dust off this book and continue from here. Thank you and have a nice day!)

As I said in the beginning of this book, although the decision to continue was easy (for some of you, at least), the path to get into the Revival Mode is a bit more difficult to handle. There are seven steps to Revival, and they are as followed:

1. *Repentance/ Responsibility*
2. *Engaging the Holy Spirit*
3. *Validation through Faith*
4. *Instilling Prayer in your Daily Life*
5. *Vanquishing Fear and Doubt*
6. *Attitude Adjustment*
7. *Living Victoriously In Christ!*

STEP ONE:

Repentance/ Responsibility

They say the first step is always the hardest of all, and in this case, it is no different. Of all the steps that I outlined earlier, this first step is a doozy! In order to repent from your sins, you must acknowledge that you are a sinner at heart. Most of us feel we are good people, and even though we may have made minor transgressions in the past, we are not so bad that God will hold us back for eternity. However, Jeremiah 19:7 said it best:

"The heart is deceitful above all things and beyond cure. Who can understand it?"

In other words, as mortal flesh, we live with wicked and deceitful hearts all our lives, and nobody can deceive God. Who, then, are we deceiving? We are deceiving ourselves! Even though we like to think we are above some of the problems that plague our world and society, we actually enable society, by our words and actions, to continue to perpetuate the hurt and pain we inflict on one another. We turn a blind eye to what's happening in the poorer parts of town, or we conveniently forget that people around the world are suffering from hunger and disease. Instead, we deceive ourselves that the problems belong to someone else, or we think by donating a few dollars will erase the hurt and pain of others. Some of us live in a fantasy world where everything is peachy and fun, and that the government will find the solutions to these problems. I'm reminded of a Don Henley video I saw when I was growing up. The song, "All She Wants to Do is Dance", takes place in a war zone of a South American country, where the protagonist, a young teenage girl, is dancing among the ruins of a bombed out village. She dances to escape the horrors and wretchedness of war, deceiving herself in the process what is really happening. Many of us are like that girl, refusing to believe we are responsible for the horrible things that plague our world and our lives.

We must do more than simply say we have sinned in order to truly repent; we must take full responsibility of how we have lived our lives up to this point. We can no longer blame our parents, our siblings, our teachers, our neighbors, or society as a whole for our own problems. We must say that we are responsible for all the hurt and pain we have endured, as well as what the world has endured. This is very difficult for many of us, because our egos will not allow us to admit we have any problems. As I said in the first section of this book, we rather be the victim than the villain of the piece. It's easier, and people don't judge us so critically. Unfortunately, God is the ultimate judge, and until you realize that his judgment is the only one you should be concerned with, then you have not truly repented. In other words, you are merely giving lip service to the Lord. Remember, God knew you before you were even formed in your mother's womb, and he can see into your heart and soul. We like to think we are so cunning, but God is far smarter than any person on the face of this planet. He can see through our wicked, deceitful ways!

Let me take this moment and say that you cannot change your wicked ways; only God can. And God can only change your ways if you let him do so. If you think that you are capable of changing who and what you are by yourself, you are truly mistaken. As big as your ego is, it will never allow you to change it on your own. You need more help, and that which God is offering is the gift of salvation. By truly repenting, and acknowledging you are responsible for all that has happened in your life, as well as accepting Jesus Christ as your Lord and Savior, then you can receive God's grace. By asking Jesus into your life, you are surrendering your ego's desires, demands, and deceitful ways to God, letting go of the pain and suffering that went with it. You are giving God control over your life at this point! Do you think you can do this? This is very difficult for people to do, and only you can choose to do so. Right now, put this book aside and pray or meditate on what you have just read. Take a look back at your life up to this point, and see how you are responsible for your own misery and despair. Think about how your life would look like had you made different decisions in your life. Reflect how your life would be had God been in control, and not you. When you are ready, and you have given your life to Christ, then move on to the next section. Believe me, it gets a lot easier from here!

NOTES

NOTES

_____

_____

_____

_____

_____

_____

_____

_____

_____

_____

_____

_____

_____

_____

_____

_____

<u>NOTES</u>

NOTES

STEP TWO:

Engaging the Holy Spirit

Now that you have fully repented, and accepted God's grace, you are now ready to embark on a personal, intimate relationship with the Lord. God wants to have an intimate relationship with you, and he wants to work with you to get to the next level of living. To accomplish this, he sends his Holy Spirit to dwell inside you, to make whatever changes are necessary to help you achieve your goal of living to your full potentiality. Through the Holy Spirit, we are able to communicate directly to God, who wants to hear our prayers and our problems. We are to engage the spirit, by first learning God's Word, as expressed in the Bible. We are to read the Bible for answers, and we are to read about how God wants us to lead our lives. God also wants us to work with others, by learning the Word together in hopes to giving us new insights and new concepts to explore. God wants us to worship with people who share His values, and praise Him for the blessings he bestows upon us. He wants us to pray for guidance, and ask for His mercy. He wants to become the Father he was meant to be in your life.

He wants to know your dreams and desires, but he also wants you to live the life He had planned for you before you were born. He wants you to be successful, but He also wants you to carry out his Word. He wants you to love Him, but He also wants you to love yourself. In other words, God wants both of you to be on the same page! You need to seek out what God truly wants from you, as well as share with him what you want from Him. You may not always get what you want, but you should get what you need. As in the story of the Good Samaritan, where God promised the woman she will never thirst again by first seeking him, you shall never want again by engaging in a very personal and private relationship with the Lord.

NOTES

<u>NOTES</u>

NOTES

<u>NOTES</u>

_____

_____

_____

_____

_____

_____

_____

_____

_____

_____

_____

_____

_____

_____

_____

_____

_____

STEP THREE:

Validation through Faith

Faith is probably the hardest concept for a Survivor to accept. It is a paradox, really, (for those who have learned not to trust or depend on others) to learn to trust an omniscient, intangible being to help them take care of their problems. Faith in God does not come easily for a Survivor. Although we may talk about having faith, we mean we have faith in ourselves and our skills and abilities, but it doesn't extend to God. For most Survivors, at least those who believe in a supreme being, God has either let us down, or He doesn't care about what happens to us. To place our complete trust and faith in a non-corporeal being just does not make any sense.

"Trust ... but Verify"

In the early to mid-1980's, we were in the throes of the Cold War, nuclear proliferation, and what is now the legacy of Ronald Reagan. The pressure to put together a nuclear disarmament treaty with the Soviets, (especially after the failure of SALT 1 and 2,) along with the loss of several Soviet leaders to death and illness, led to the rise of Mikhail Gorbachev and his politics of Perestroika. When pressed by a reporter why, due to the changes in the Soviet system, that Reagan would not commit to a treaty that Gorbachev offered to him. Reagan, in his own inimitable style, proceeded to explain his actions. Even though he trusted Gorbachev and the new Soviet leadership, he wanted to have some form of accountability of their disarmament programs. This would become his doctrine of *"Trust But Verify"*.

In many respects, we treat God in the same manner; we believe in God, but we want proof of His love for us before we begin trusting in absolute faith. We survivors have been burned in the past, and we don't want to put ourselves out in the future. Unfortunately, that is not how

God works. God already proved His love for us by giving up His only son, Jesus Christ, for our sins. He doesn't have to do any more. Instead, He expects you to walk and act in faith, and then he will give his blessings if he so chooses. Hence, the Paradox.

The Book of Romans clearly explains this paradox in greater detail. The apostle Paul writes in Romans, Chapter One, about God's wrath against mankind. In Romans 1:20, he spells out that "for since the creation of the world God's invisible qualities - His eternal power and divine nature - have been clearly seen, so that men are without excuse." Even though this truth was evident, "men have suppressed the truth by their wickedness" (Romans 1:19). In other words, God allowed us to continue to live in sin and depravity because of our lack of faith. Paul continues to caution others, by telling his followers that on "the day of God's wrath, when his judgment will be revealed, God will give to each person according to what he has done." (Romans 2:5,6) In other words, as you continue to live by your stubborn, unrepentant ways, you are only hurting yourself in the end. God is to be praised and worshipped for all He has done for us. We should be more appreciative of all the things He does in our lives, even those things in which we find the hardest to understand. As believers, we have to understand that he is preparing us for His kingdom, and that we may never see the full blessings He has planned for us. The Book of Hebrews makes this clearer for us to understand. In Chapter 11, from Abraham to Moses to David and the prophets, God has asked these men to act in faith and even though some have perished before their work was done, their blessings came to later generations. As stated in Hebrews 11:1-3, "Faith is being sure of what we hope for and certain of what we do not see. This is what the ancients were commended for. By faith, we understand that the universe was formed at God's command, so that what is seen was not made out of what was visible."

Faith finds its foundation in our relationship with God. As stated earlier in this book, God seeks to have a personal relationship with us, and once we establish this relationship, he will reward our faith with blessings. He wants you to initiate the relationship with Him. He wants you to pray to Him and worship Him. We were created for the express purpose of worshipping God, not the other way around. This reminds me of an amusing story I heard about regarding dogs and cats. It goes like this:

The Difference between Dogs and Cats

This is a story of a dog and a cat who live in the same home together. Every morning, their caregiver feeds them a nutritious meal. The dog begins thinking to himself, "The caregiver feeds me, bathes me, and keeps me safe and secure in this house. I am so lucky! He must be a god!" The cat of the house also begins to reflect on her caregiver, "The caregiver feeds me, bathes me, and keeps me safe and secure in this house. I am so lucky! I must be a god!"

In many respects, we Survivors act like the cat in this story, that God should be catering to our needs, when in fact, we should be more like the dog in the story, as he is more appreciative of his caregiver, and wants to do whatever it takes to please him. Only by showing our love and appreciation for God will he validate our faith by rewarding us with His Blessings. We must be mindful of what God has done for us in the past, and what he plans to do for us in the future. God has expectations from you as well. He wants us to be part of His glorious mission, to bring others like ourselves to Him. As we carry out His plans for us, he will provide for us and be present in us through the Holy Spirit. That is His promise!

Jesus describes faith to be like a mustard seed. As a seed, it is very small, yet when planted, it grows to be the largest of plants. For a Survivor, he or she only has to have the smallest bit of faith, and it will grow larger within him or her as time goes on. In my own case, I used to say to myself, "My faith grows stronger every day, in every way." Now my faith is unshakable, even in the most trying of situations. You only need to start small, and you too will watch your faith grow as well.

NOTES

<u>NOTES</u>

NOTES

_____

_____

_____

_____

_____

_____

_____

_____

_____

_____

_____

_____

_____

_____

_____

_____

NOTES

STEP FOUR:

Instilling Prayer Into Your Life

As stated in the last section, Faith finds its foundation in our relationship with God. As such, Prayer is the foundational beginning point of direct and open communication with God. Prayer plays a critical role in the Revival process, as it is as essential to a believer as prayer nourishes the soul the same way as food nourishes the body. It is unhealthy for us to be without either food or prayer. It is our source of spiritual energy. When we are in Survival mode, we tend to forget about the power of prayer in our life, instead opting to try to do things ourselves. That's why we find ourselves worn down, burnt out, and fatigued to the bone. In order for Revival to take place, we must take a more conscientious look at prayer in our lives.

Let me state from the onset that I am, by no means or stretch of the imagination, a Prayer Warrior. As a Survivor, when and if I did pray, I would do a more formulaic prayer, usually ending in a request from God for assistance. The prayer would be short and to the point, but usually the prayer would go unanswered. However, I have learned what I was doing wrong in my prayer life, and as a consequence, I have begun to change my approach to prayer and meditation. In fact, I recommend reading the book, **How to Develop a Powerful Prayer Life**, by Dr. Gregory R. Frizzell. It's a short book (like this one), and could be read in a few short sittings. His insights are profound, and he believes anybody could have a powerful prayer life, if it is so desired.

Before we begin to explore what a prayer life looks like, we have to know what it doesn't look like. First of all, prayer should not be seen as just some form of religious activity, one that you are obligated to perform. Many Christians have a short, rote prayer they recite, believing that is all God wants to hear. The problem with these prayers is they sound and feel mechanical and empty, devoid of any substance. Second of all, prayers should not be a spiritual laundry list of areas that you want God to fix in your life. Too often, people view prayer as a time to unload all of your problems on God. Third of all, prayer time should not just be some form of spiritual wish list, where we ask God for spiritual things, and in return, we will do His bidding. According to the book, **Made to Count**, by Bob Reccord and Randy Singer, there are three purposes for an intimate prayer life:

1. **To mode and shape you to be like Him,**
2. **For you to participate with God in the work He wants to do,**
3. **And to reveal to you what He is planning to do so you can adjust your life to Him and join his work.**

Dr. Frizzell, in his book, talks about the need to have a balanced prayer life. In order for your prayer life to be balanced, you must partake in five different prayer types, which are:

1. *Praise, Thanksgiving and Worship* (daily adoration and worship)
2. *Confession and Repentance* (receiving God's forgiveness)
3. *Petition and Supplication* (presenting our individual needs to others)
4. *Intercession* (focus on the needs of others)
5. *Meditation* (listening prayer and reflection)

Dr. Frizzell suggests that our prayer life should balance all five of these prayer types in our daily routine if we are to become spiritual strong. He compares it to an unbalanced diet, which can eventually weaken you if you are not careful. Similarly, your prayer life should constitute all five types, not just one or two, if you are to become spiritually strong. I strongly suggest that you read Dr. Frizzell's book, as well as the book, **Made to Count**, to assist you in becoming stronger in prayer than you are right now. If you seek to have a strong relationship with the Father, then you must develop your prayer life. As my former pastor said at one of his sermons, "No one's relationship with Christ will ever rise above the level of his or her prayer life!" Remember, prayer is not what we can get from God, but to bring Glory to God.

I would suggest that the next time you pray, simply have a conversation with God. It does not have to be elaborate or convoluted, but sincere and open. Tell him your thoughts, your feelings, and your concerns. Ask him for clarity and peace of mind. Start small, and then watch your prayers (and your faith) become validated. It may be difficult at first (it was for me), but over time, it will become second nature, almost like breathing and sleeping. I am telling you, prayer works!

<u>NOTES</u>

_____

_____

_____

_____

_____

_____

_____

_____

_____

_____

_____

_____

_____

_____

_____

_____

NOTES

<u>**NOTES**</u>

NOTES

STEP FIVE:

Vanquishing Fear and Doubt!

Remember that deceiving heart we talked about earlier? Well, even though you have repented, as well as begun a relationship with God, your ego wants to get back into the driver's seat again, and he uses the only tool he has in his arsenal to get there. That tool is Fear! Fear, to me, is like a Swiss Army Knife, a single tool with many different kinds of attachments. Fear will use deception, discouragement, hatred, anger, and anything else in its sheath to get you to allow the ego to control you once more. The ego only lives for one thing and one thing only; its own gratification. It doesn't matter if it leads you to a life of struggle and heart ache, as long as it is in control of your life! Fear will rear its ugly head by filling you up with doubts and apprehensions and disappointments.

Let me use myself as an example. After I initially repented of my sins, I was besieged by nightmares. Even though I had been saved, these nightmares reared their ugly heads, trying to get to see the errors of my ways. The ego wanted to regain the ground it had just lost, and started to invade my nightmares with the fears and apprehensions that dominated my Survivor lifestyle. My dreams were telling me that I shouldn't limit myself to one religion, or one school of thought. My dreams were telling me that my debts and my "responsibilities" should be my priorities, not God. Eventually, I could not sleep at night, as the fears overcame me. I would wake up in the middle of the night, filled with worry and despair as I needed to figure out how I was going to pay my bills. I began to question my decision to seek salvation, as the price seemed too high.

Another thing that happened shortly after I was baptized was that I was exposed to other religions and other schools of thought. I began to wonder if I had made the correct decision after all. Who was to say which religion was the best for me? My friends, who belonged to these churches, would invite me to visit their churches. I did, and it only served to confuse me more and more. Many preached the same gospel, but each had their own takes on things. Being inexperienced in the ways of religion, I was afraid I may not have made the right choice after all Fear, doubt, uncertainty, worry, and panic soon settled in. This is what I considered too high a price for me. When I was agnostic, I was fine. I lived my life accordingly, and I did not bother anybody. Now that I was saved, I was constantly stressing out over my choices and decisions, and worried about the consequences. There was no possible way to live up to God's high standards, and I would fail and let him down. Even worse, I thought God would turn his back to me, forsaking me forever. That's a scary thought in itself!

These thoughts were unsettling, to say the least. This led me to dream a very revealing dream, which led me to the Book of Luke. In Luke, Chapter 8, Jesus shares with his disciples the Parable of the Sower, in which he compares spreading the word of God with a sower spreading seeds across the land. The seed, Jesus said, is the word of God. The word is heard by everyone, but there are those who hear, but do nothing about it. There are those like the rock, who receive the word with joy when they hear it, but they do not take root. They believe it for awhile, but in the time of testing they fall away. A seed that falls among the thorns stands for those who hear, but as they go on their way they are choked by life's worries, riches and pleasures, so they do not mature. The seed that falls on good soil stand for those with noble and good hearts, who hear the word, retain it, and by persevering produce a crop. I don't know about you, but I felt like I fit somewhere between the rock and the thorns. My own fears and doubts were choking off any kind of maturation that should be taken place within me. Anyway, I told my friend this revelation, and he pointed out to me another parable in Mark Chapter 6; v.25-34. In this parable, Jesus tells us not to worry, as God is the great provider, and even though the birds do not store food away for a rainy day, God will always provide for them, and that we should consider ourselves more valuable to

Him than a bird. He also tells us that we should first seek his kingdom and his righteousness, and all these things will be given to you as well. He finishes by telling us that we should not worry about tomorrow, for tomorrow will worry about itself. He reminds us that each day has enough trouble of its own. In other words, we should cast off our worries and doubts and leave them to God.

FDR said it best; "The only thing to fear is Fear itself." The Bible is full of stories of God telling his prophets not to fear, but to put their trust in Him. The Book of Psalms was written while David was being chased by those trying to destroy him. Yet he put his trust in God that his life would be spared and that his enemies will be defeated. This takes a whole lot of courage, in the face of unmitigated terror. God wants us to trust Him, to put our faith in Him, to provide for us. When we become part of the body of Christ, he will do whatever it takes to keep us safe and secure in the Kingdom. The truth is that we no longer need to live in fear, as long as we put our faith in God's merciful arms. Once we can come to terms with this concept, our lives will be easier to handle. The problem is that as Survivors, we have learned that we can not depend on anybody but ourselves, and we look to ourselves to solve the problem at hand. I liken it to a person who has leaky pipes. Instead of finding a plumber, who may charge them hundreds of dollars to fix the pipes, the person decides to fix them himself. Using unorthodox methods, the pipes may be fixed for a time, but then other problems begin to develop. Other parts of the pipe begin to leak, and before long, the whole pipe bursts, flooding the basement! This now winds up costing thousands of dollars, as we now have an even greater problem than before. We have to see God as the Master Plumber, who can repair it all as long as we put our problems in his hands before they spin out of control. All it takes is a little faith! Just put your full trust and faith in God, and your fears will soon be vanquished.

NOTES

<u>NOTES</u>

NOTES

NOTES

_____

_____

_____

_____

_____

_____

_____

_____

_____

_____

_____

_____

_____

_____

_____

_____

STEP SIX:

Attitude Adjustment

What is an attitude? An attitude is a like or dislike, a positive or negative evaluation about some aspect of the world. When someone is living in Survivor mode, that person's attitude toward life was pretty negative, for the most part. I would like for you to take time to reflect about how you were thinking while living in your Survival mode. You were selfish; unfocused and undisciplined; you reacted to your environment; you were subject to volatile mood swings; you were full of apprehension and fear; and you suffered from low self-esteem, as you began doubting yourself. Now, if you have been following the steps described in the Revival section in this book, you have gone through some tremendous changes. First, you have taken responsibility for everything that has happened in your life up to this point, and repented for your sins. Secondly, you have asked God to send in the Holy Spirit to do good work in your heart. Thirdly, you began walking in faith, and you have instilled prayer into your life. Lastly, you have found the courage and faith to vanquish fear and doubt from your life once and for all. Now you are ready to go to the next step, which my dear friend, Barbara, affectionately calls "Doing the Love Walk".

What does the Love Walk look like for you? As Paul states in the Book of Romans (Chapter 8), when we live according to our sinful, worldly nature, the sinful mind is hostile to God. (Romans 8:7) This is because we live in fear of God. As Survivors, we are always living in fear, constantly afraid of what lurks behind every corner. As sinners, those controlled by their sinful nature cannot please God. (Romans 8:8) However, as Paul states, when we live in accordance to the spirit (and not the flesh), the mind controlled by the spirit is life and peace, (Romans 8:6) for you did not receive a spirit that makes you a slave again to fear, but you received the Spirit of sonship (Romans 8:15). You are now a part of the body of Christ, and as such, walking in love takes on a whole new meaning for you. Paul would later discuss this in the 1 Corinthians, when he describes to the disciples just what love is. In 1 Corinthians (13: 4 - 8), Paul describes love like this;

Love is patient, love is kind.
It does not envy, it does not boast, it is not proud.
It is not rude, it is not self-seeking,
It is not easily angered, it keeps no record of wrongs.
Love does not delight in evil but rejoices in Truth.
It always protects, always trusts, always hopes, always perseveres.
Love never fails.

When you are walking in love, you will notice your attitude towards others have changed. You are no longer acting selfishly, or behaving arrogantly or rudely. You are not frustrated or quick tempered. You no longer react to the minor irritations that surface in your life. You are no longer deceitful and manipulative, using insincere flattery or setting up scenarios to make yourself look good. You no longer feel competitive to those around you, coveting what your neighbors, friends, and family members have. You no longer feel like a victim, but that you are part of a very special group of believers living in Christ. You have been, and currently are being, changed from the inside out. It is a daily process and you need the leadership of the Holy Spirit to help keep you on track and in focus. You need to hear your instructions in reading and studying the Word in your heart, not just in your head. By reflecting and meditating on the Word of God, which is Truth, you will slowly see your attitudes about life change for the better. This leads us directly to the next step on our journey ...

NOTES

_____

_____

_____

_____

_____

_____

_____

_____

_____

_____

_____

_____

_____

_____

_____

_____

_____

_____

<u>NOTES</u>

NOTES

<u>**NOTES**</u>

STEP SEVEN:

Living Victoriously in Christ

You are now ready to ascend to the next level, beyond mere sustenance and survival. You are ready to live life to its fullest potential, the kind of life God designed for you. You have learned to pray and meditate. You have learned to act in faith. You have stared Fear directly in the eye and shouted "No More!". You have adjusted your internal settings, and now you are prepared to go further than you had ever thought possible. You are ready to Live Victoriously in Christ! Hallelujah! Glory be to God!

To understand what living in Christ looks like, it's best to go directly to the Source. In John 15:1-5, Jesus tells his disciples just how this looks for you and me:

"I am the true vine, and my Father is the gardener. He cuts off every branch in me that bears no fruit, while every branch that does bear fruit he prunes so that it will be more fruitful. You are already clean because of the word I have spoken to you. Remain in me, and I will remain in you. No branch can bear fruit by itself; it must remain in the vine. Neither can you bear fruit unless you remain in me.

"I am the vine; you are the branches. If a man remains in me and I in him, he will bear much fruit; apart from me you can do nothing."

What a powerful statement! What Jesus is saying here is that apart from him, your successes will be limited and few, if any. However, with Jesus on your side, you will have more success than you ever had, and you will bear more fruit than ever before. I know this for a fact. I have tried, over these many years, to create big projects that will lead to fame and fortune for myself. Unfortunately, fate always dealt me a bad hand, and my projects would literally "die on the vine." Now, my calling is to write, to teach, and to coach others. I no longer desire fame or fortune. All the glory shall go to God. I just want to do my part to help the Kingdom grow and expand. I feel God is preparing me, even as I am writing these words. I have wrote books in the past, but they have never gone anywhere. Now, I am in the process of writing 5 completely different books! I am finally doing what God wants me to do!

You have to constantly put God first in everything you do. He has a plan for you, and He wants to help you complete those tasks. If you ever think you can do it alone, you will fail. God is the Master Planner of the universe, and He knows just what He needs you to do. He will give you the gifts and the skills necessary to help you complete your mission. If you do not have a skill or gift, He will bring someone to you to assist you in your endeavor. I have been helped enormously by the people in my church with this book, especially when it comes to Scripture. You see, I am still learning as well, and as I said before, it is a continual process.

When you finally realize that God is in control, it gives one a sense of peace. No longer do you have to feel like it's you against the world. No longer do you have to feel like you are trying to swim upstream. It is such a liberating feeling, as now you can concentrate on those areas in which you can excel. By putting your trust and faith in God, you no longer have to keep looking over your shoulder in fear. You do not realize how much energy and time we waste when we live with worry or fear. As Jesus states in Luke 12:25-26, "Who of you by worrying can add a single hour to his life? Since you cannot do this very little thing, why do you worry about the rest?" If I could get back all the time I lost to fear and worry, I'd probably have another life time! However, as a Survivor, this is usually the norm than the exception. However, with God in control, the Survivor can now begin to live his or her life in earnest for the Lord. I believe Paul said it best in Romans 5:1, "It is for freedom that Christ has set us free.

Stand firm, then, and do not let yourselves be burdened by a yoke of slavery!"

Many people are probably asking at this time, just what are the 'fruits' that Jesus was talking about before? Paul describes the fruit of the Spirit as being "love, joy, peace, patience, kindness, goodness, faithfulness, gentleness and self-control. Against such things there is no law" (Galatians 5:22-23) He further went on to say that "those who belong to Christ have crucified their sinful nature with its passions and desires. Since we live by the Spirit, let us keep in step with the Spirit." (Galatians 5:25) In other words, we should concentrate our efforts on God's mission, and not our own personal agendas. Many Christians claim that they are spiritual, but they continue to live by worldly standards. The more we stay in step with the Spirit, as Paul commanded, the more fruitful we become in all the areas of our lives. And the more fruitful we become, the more victorious we live in Christ! Amen to that!

<u>NOTES</u>

NOTES

NOTES

NOTES

CONCLUSION

While sitting here at my computer, trying to find the best way to end this book, I was suddenly reminded of an old bumper sticker I saw back in the '80's. Just what did this sticker say? *POVERTY SUCKS!* Direct, to the point, and unfortunately, very true. Living in Survival mode all the time is very much like living in poverty. Being a Survivor is not heroic, nor is it fun or glamorous. It taxes you emotionally, physically, and spiritually. You become drained by all the worry and anxiety that besets you. I firmly believe that being a Survivor is akin to being spiritually impoverished, without hope and without mercy. To this, I would say that *SURVIVAL SUCKS!*

As much as I disdain living like a Survivor, it is important to realize that there is an alternative. God designed us to live with purpose and passion in our lives, and only Satan wants to keep us trapped in the Survival mode. God has a way for you to spring from this trap, and that is REVIVAL! He wants us to live happy, fulfilling lives, and if you take the steps we discussed during this last part of the book, you too can feel that joy and excitement of living life to its fullest potential. Not only is it what you truly desire, but it is what God desires as well.

Is it easy? Nothing worth doing ever comes easy. Is it worth it? You better believe it is. My life has drastically changed while writing this book, and yours will, too, if you are willing to apply the principles offered here. While it can be difficult, especially for those with hardened hearts and closed minds, the true worth cannot be measured. It would take another whole book to describe in detail what is being offered through Revival. My goal here was to get you to recognize how limited your life is without the Lord's involvement in it. Once you were able to recognize and accept the Truth, then you can make the necessary adjustments in your life to turn it around. It is my hope that everyone reading this book gets Revival in their lives, and go into newer, more powerful directions for themselves. So, break free of your limited existence, and break through to new heights of living joyfully and purposefully. And remember .... **_REVIVAL RULES!_** (Maybe I should print up some bumper stickers...just a thought!)

About the Author

Joseph Pero is an adopted son of God and a follower of Jesus Christ. He is also an experienced financial consultant, with over 6 years of experience helping people with their debt and credit problems. He is the owner of Premier Money Management Solutions, which helps people eliminate their debt and build wealth. He resides in Cleveland, Ohio, and has two cats, Belle and Kari.

NOTES

NOTES

NOTES

NOTES

NOTES

NOTES

NOTES

NOTES